THE GREEN LAKE IS AWAKE

SELECTED POEMS BY JOSEPH CERAVOLO

The Green Lake Is Awake

EDITORS: LARRY FAGIN, KENNETH KOCH, CHARLES NORTH,

RON PADGETT, DAVID SHAPIRO, & PAUL VIOLI

COFFEE HOUSE PRESS :: MINNEAPOLIS :: 1994

Cover art by Nora L. Koch

These works first appeared in the following: *Fits of Dawn*, C Press; *Wild Flowers Out of Gas*, Tibor De Nagy; *Spring in This World of Poor Mutts*, Columbia University Press; *Transmigration Solo*, Toothpaste Press; *Millennium Dust*, Kulchur; *An Anthology of New York Poets*, Random House; *Locus Solus* magazine; and *Art and Literature* magazine.

The publishers regret any omissions and will gladly include unmentioned publications in future editions.

The publishers would like to thank Z Press for assistance with this project. We would also like to thank the Minnesota State Arts Board for a general operating support grant through an appropriation by the Minnesota State Legislature. Major new marketing initiatives have been made possible by the Lila Wallace–Reader's Digest Literary Publishers Marketing Development Program, funded through a grant to the Council of Literary Magazines and Presses.

Coffee House Press books are available to the trade through our primary distributor, Consortium Book Sales & Distribution, 1045 Westgate Drive, Saint Paul, MN 55114. Our books are also available through all major library distributors and jobbers, and through most small press distributors. For personal orders, catalogs, or other information, write to:
Coffee House Press
27 North Fourth Street, Suite 400, Minneapolis, MN 55401

Library of Congress Cataloging-in-Publication Data
Ceravolo, Joseph, 1934–1988
  The green lake is awake : selected poems / by Joseph Ceravolo.
    p.   cm.
  ISBN 978-1-56689-021-2
    1. Nature—Poetry.   I. Title.
  PS3553.E7G7 1994   93-23692
  811'.54—dc20   CIP

10   9   8   7   6   5   4   3   2

CONTENTS

9   Introduction by Kenneth Koch

15 Dusk

16 It Is Morning

17 Caught in the Swamp

18 Heart Feels the Water

19 Lighthouse

20 The Wind Is Blowing West

22 Warmth

23 Cool Breeze

24 Ocean

25 White Fish in Reeds

26 Ho Ho Ho Caribou

31 Red Sun

32 Indian Suffering

33 Fill and Illumined

34 Passivation

38 Passion for the Sky

39 Pregnant, I Come

40 Spring in This World of Poor Mutts

43 Data

44 A Song of Autumn

45 Autumn Break

46 I Like to Collapse

47 Down

48 Autumn-Time, Wind and the Planet Pluto

49 Soul in Migration

51 Drunken Winter

52 Wild Provoke of the Endurance Sky

53 Struggling

54 Grow

55 Dangers of the Journey to the Happy Land

56 Risk

57 Happiness in the Trees

58 Fly

59 The Book of Wild Flowers

60 In My Crib

61 Don't Break It

62 Spring

63 Book III from *Fits of Dawn*

78 Water: How Weather Feels the Cotton Hotels

91 Contrast

92 Floating Gardens

93 O Heart Uncovered

94 Pain Songs

100 Migratory Noon

101 Chains of Mountains

102 Note from St. Francis

103 Cross Fire

104 Fire of Myself

105 Star Song

106 Sea Level

117 Grass

118 Route

119 May

120 The Green Lake Is Awake

ON THE POETRY OF JOSEPH CERAVOLO

Modern poetry takes a large step in this poetry that has not yet
really been followed by others. It is as if one could see the print
of that step in the snow, and then a great beautiful snowy wil-
derness but no more tracks. In this respect it resembles the
work of such poets as John Wheelwright or Gerard Manley
Hopkins, its stylistic innovations so bound up with the expres-
sion of a particular sensibility as to be, even though inspiring,
inimitable.

Ceravolo's poetic subject is often a moment, caught, as it
were, off guard and open to all kinds of other moments and
their sensations:

> Then there is nothing   think!
> the angular explanation
> boom!   he was a parade
>   with a gift
> a question cable of
>   thought
> a thermos savage in
>   the hotel
> in vera cruz color
>   sand the boat

This is not "just language" (no such remarkable description as
that of a man as "a parade with a gift" could be that), but de-
scriptive language arranged and disarranged in such a way as
to keep the feelings and ideas fixed in it, fresh and sharp, every
time the passage is read. What these lines say, in a prose way,
doesn't make sense in an ordinary way—a human being is not
(not without further explanation, in any case) a parade, a cable,
or a thermos savage. But what the lines suggest (which is what

they say if you take them on what might be termed "poetic faith") makes sense of a kind that is found only in poetry. Another example of a Ceravolo "moment," from this same poem ("Water: How Weather Feels the Cotton Hotels") has a more concentrated, almost microscopic intensity, while at the same time seeming quite large and open:

> earthenware
> drawing its own
> tonight on some
> particular wasp

I knew Joseph Ceravolo and his poems for twenty-five years. He would send me a poem like "How Weather Feels the Cotton Hotels," and, every time, I'd gasp. It was wonderful and I didn't know how he had done it. It faded like the mirage of a gorgeous building; then, as soon as I reread it, it was there again. What was Ceravolo doing? Whatever it was, somehow in four lines he brought me intense, clear feelings of wasps on earthenware, of nights, of feelings wasps must have, that clay pots might have. A new—or, rather, old but unlighted—part of my experience was given light. His poems were a sort of amazing perceptual archeology.

Rather than explaining ("Seeing this wasp landing . . .") or conventional poeticizing ("O wasp alighting!"), which risks making such moments banal or false, Ceravolo's method uses indirection, rapid transitions, dissociation, and other kinds of apparent "nonsense." These oddnesses are there not to be resolved but to be given in to, so that the poem can have its say. If one can do that, it's certainly worth it.

There are, in this poetry pairs of seemingly unconnected words—"rice Spring", "Sail glooms", "boom autumn"; and seemingly unconnected phrases and lines—"As far as I look we are across A/ boat crosses by. There is no monkey in me/ left:

Sleep." There are many odd usages, words put together in "incorrect" ways—"These are my clothes to a/ boat"—and syntactically unfinished statements:

> Hold me
> Till only,   these are my
>   clothes   I sit.

These oddnesses take place in a context of simplicity, quietness, and directness. They aren't avant-garde explosions for their own sake, but occur when they are necessary to the difficult, exciting expressions of whatever has to be said.

> There's nothing to love in this
> rice Spring.
> Collected something warm like friends.
> Sail glooms are none . . .

One could sing this. One would know well enough what it meant.

Ceravolo was influenced by William Carlos Williams, sometimes, though his poetry goes elsewhere. In the work of both there is a blurring expansion of identity, a sort of giving oneself completely to a tree, an insect, flowers. Williams' aim, in such poems as "Daisy," "Queen Anne's Lace," and "The Young Sycamore," is usually accomplished in his merging with the thing observed so as to describe it more convincingly. Ceravolo has a tendency to go back and forth from one identity to another:

> I am a dirty little bug
> Plants!, because
> I'm small   because there's no courage
> in me   will you come home

with me? And
stay   With us on the bed

When Ceravolo, like Williams, is merely looking, he can be trusted to say what is right there, in the simplest, most direct manner—"man walking with his/ shoulders haunched and tufts/ of white duck hair in the back/ of the head!"; when he goes beyond ordinary perceptions, this atmosphere of accuracy stays with him. It is a quality rare among poets, a combination of clear down-to-earthness with the sort of wild dreaminess of Lorca or Rimbaud, as in this passage from "May":

Morning oh May flower! oh
May exist. Built.
When will water stop ·
Cooling? Built, falling. Reeds. I am surprised . . .

After the excited, ambiguous invocation (of May), a number of profound ideas are suggested with surprising simplicity and speed: the notion that the month of May has been "Built"; the wondering if water will keep its qualities; the realization that water also has been built, and built, probably, so as to be falling (even falling things are built). After this there is a return to plain physical presence, a fact ("reeds") and plain everyday consciousness ("I am surprised"). Ceravolo's work is full of pleasures like these. Sometimes his sensations are expressed in language that seems as physical as the things he is talking about:

Oak oak! like like
it then
    cold some wild paddle
so sky then . . .

Even the most simply descriptive poems about something seen have a characteristic lift:

> The fish are staying here
> and eating. The plant is
> thin and has very long leaves
> like insects' legs, the way
> they bend down.
> Through the water
> the plant breaks from the water:
>
> the line of the water and the air.
> Told!

The slowed-down, superimposed perceptions of lines 6, 7, and 8 are extraordinary and all Ceravolo's own.

To read these poems is to be refreshed and surprised. They are the real thing. Their audience may always be limited by one of their great qualities: they are aesthetically uncompromising, and make no gestures or appeals outside themselves. Anyone lucky enough to read them, however, will have one of the great true experiences of twentieth-century poetry.

—Kenneth Koch

DUSK

Before the dusk grows deeper
Now comes a little moth dressed in
rose pink, wings bordered with yellow. Now
a tiger moth, now another and another   another

IT IS MORNING

Too late
Hard fish
Too late to be morning
Too early . . . . . early love
The tree played into
by 4 birds
The hornet . . . . . even though
the nest is shaking
Where did they go?

CAUGHT IN THE SWAMP

High is the dark clouds
and the harbor and
the egg as the antelope
frightens us through the
swampy harbor. We burn
our food, and the egg
has a seal of abandon
        in its blueness.
Which are we humming at last?
It is the running of the shiny antelope
we smell, not love.
Is it the bed?

HEART FEELS THE WATER

The fish are staying here
and eating. The plant is
thin and has very long leaves
like insects' legs, the way
they bend down.
Through the water
the plant breaks from the water:

the line of the water and the air.
Told!

LIGHTHOUSE

All this summer fun.
The big waves, and waiting
(the moon is broken)
for the moon to come out
and revive the water. You look
and you want to watch as
men feel the beer breaking
on their lips, and women seem like
the sun on your little back.
Where are you closer to everything?
in the plants? on the photograph or
the little heart that's not
used to beating like the waves' foam?
       A wasp is
looking for a hole in the screen.
No. There's no man in the lighthouse.
There's no woman there, but there is
a light there; it is a bulb.
And I think how complete you are
in its light. Flash . . . . Flash . . . . .
. . . .
And I think of how our room
will smell; You lying on one bed
and we in the other,
facing the . . . flash . . . . .
. . . . Flash

THE WIND IS BLOWING WEST

I

I am trying to decide to go swimming,
But the sea looks so calm.
All the other boys have gone in.
I can't decide what to do.

I've been waiting in my tent
Expecting to go in.
Have you forgotten to come down?
Can I escape going in?
I was just coming

I was just going in
But lost my pail

2

A boisterous tide is coming up;
I was just looking at it.
The pail is near me
again. My shoulders have sand on them.

Round the edge of the tide
Is the shore. The shore
Is filled with waves.
They are tin waves.

Boisterous tide coming up.
The tide is getting less.

3

Daytime is not a brain,
Living is not a cricket's song.
Why does light diffuse
As earth turns away from the sun?

I want to give my food
To a stranger. I want
to be taken.
What kind of a face do

I have while leaving?
I'm thinking of my friend.

4

I am trying to go swimming
But the sea looks so calm
All boys are gone
I can't decide what to do

I've been waiting to go
Have you come down?
Can I escape

I am just coming
        Just going in

WARMTH

There's nothing to love in this
rice Spring.
Collected something warm like friends.
Sail glooms are none.
Your desire
rests like sailors in
their bunks. Have beaten you, lips.
Supply me
man made keeping.
Supply it flowing out;
are brute bullets in your back
because there is
in this rice Spring

COOL BREEZE

In the night
in the day
it's possible to be defeated,
but how I love.
We walk down.
The children feel warm
but where is defeat?
I look up
The sun is
on the wet glass. The beach
where I love is now cool.
The children are still warm.

OCEAN

I paid you off.
  Now I want you to steal me.
My eyes are full of cement.
Wherever I am
when everything's so fated.
"I know I couldn't sleep"

Meet me wherever I am,
because I paid off,
even though I couldn't sleep.
And frighten them away.
I couldn't sleep, but a new
wave comes every few seconds.

Yes! they end on the shore.

WHITE FISH IN REEDS

Hold me
till only,   these are my
        clothes   I sit.
Give them   more songs than
the flower
These are my clothes to a
boat   Streets
have no feeling
Clouds move

Are people woman?
Who calls you
on a sun shirt sleeves down his ecstasy
The hair you are
becoming? Mmmm

That this temperate is where
I feed   The sheep sorrel flower is
And I want to
be
among all things
that bloom
Although I do not
love flowers

HO HO HO CARIBOU

for Rosemary

1

Leaped at the caribou.
My son looked at the caribou.
The kangaroo leaped on the
fruit tree. I am a white
man and my children
are hungry
which is like paradise.
The doll is sleeping.
It lay down to creep into
the plate.
It was clean and flying.

2

Where you . . . . the axes
are. Why is this home so
hard. So much
like the sent over the
courses below the home
having a porch.

Felt it on my gate in the place
where caribous jumped
over. Where geese sons
and pouches of daughters look at
me and say "I'm hungry
daddy."

3

Not alone in the
gastrous   desert. We are looking
at the caribous out in the water
swimming around. We
want to go in the ocean
along the dunes.
Where do we like?
    Like little lice in the sand
we look into a fruit expanse.
Oh the sky is so cold.
We run into the water.
Lice in heaven.

4

My heel. Ten o'clock the class.
Underwater fish
brush by us. Oh leg
not reaching!
The show is stopping
at the sky to drive in the
truck. Tell us where to
stop and eat. And
drink which comes to us out
in the sand is
                at a star.
My pants are damp.
Is tonight treating us
but not reaching through the window.

5

Where is that bug going?
Why are your hips
rounded as the sand?
What is jewelry?

Baby sleeps. Sleeping on
the cliff is dangerous.
The television of all voice is
way far behind.
Do we flow nothing?
Where did you follow that bug
to?
     See quick . . . . . . is flying.

6

Caribou, what have I
done? See how her
heart moves like a little
bug . . . . . . under my thumb.
Throw me deeply.
I am the floes.
Ho ho ho caribou,
light brown and wetness
caribou. I stink and
I know it.
"Screw you! . . . . you're right."

7

Everyone has seen us out
with the caribou but
no one has seen us out in
the car. You passed
beyond us.
We saw your knees
but the other night we
couldn't call you.
You were more far than a
widow feeling you.
Nothing has been terrible.
We are the people who have
been running with
animals.
More than when we run?

8

Tell us where o eat to stop and eat.
The diner is never gonna come.
The forest things are passing.
I did drink my milk
like a mother of wolves.
Wolves on the desert
of ice cold love, of
fireproof breasts and the breast
I took like snow.
Following me
I love you
and I fall beyond
and I eat you like a
bow and arrow withering in the
        desert.

9

No one should be mean.
Making affection and all the green
winters wide awake.
Blubber is desert. Out on
the firm lake, o firm
and aboriginal kiss.
To dance, to hunt, to sing,
no one should be mean.
Not needing these things.

10

Like a flower, little light, you open
and we make believe
we die. We die all around
you like a snake in a
well and we come up out
of the warm well and
are born again out of dry
mammas, nourishing mammas, always
holding you as I
love you and am
revived inside you, but
die in you and am
never born again in
the same place; never
stop!

RED SUN

You can't take me with a look.
These are the keys
to an orgy

after work
but they will not work
of beautiful sensuality.

Yes, work is so remote, here beneath the tides

I cannot plant the creep's
universe   As my hair stands
out   of one autumn chance
to another   O

The late red sun
farther than the equinox of a dream,
cannot make the people
more vivid than this goddess's eye.

INDIAN SUFFERING

Look, ah, dry
streets, still
not a gorged begin, he time in
you love,
cruel. What are
we doing to our faces? He waits
to grow up. Who
are you when you don't grow? Would it
mean to usually
range animal things that
satisfy? Is nature a day begun?
Bow wow wow I am
going home.
The children called
him ugly boy. I am not
afraid of
anything. Boy-not-afraid.
Ugly boy a magic.

FILL AND ILLUMINED

God created his image.
I love him like the door.
Speak to me now.
Without god there is no god.
Forget everything!
Lie down and be circumscribed
         and circumcised.
Yet there is no pain.
Yet there is no joy.

PASSIVATION

IF THE CORRODING

I

O great world that trains me! that loses my
head in the balance of coordination, even when
I'm ripe. I sting myself.

O warm world, O green ragged blood   of after dawn
as we come out singing to hear some evening birds sing.

There's no use to ask me to mind the nest,
I forget. Why do you live in the lapwing marshes?

MEDIUM REACTS WITH

2

Is there a morning moon?
A fresh wind moon?
I could hate (love) Therefore hide me . . . . Hide . . .
going to warmness
Disease is thinking in the
sand You were born
I am a little dirty bug
Plants!, because
I'm small because there's no courage
in me   will you come home
with me? And
stay With us on the bed

Like snowflakes on the ice.

THE METAL

3

O beautiful pale seagull who
stands near the trucks and
tractors and when they
start, looks around
surprised and turns (into whose wings open
from him) and change

Why do we invade
    as the peas are ripe as the beans
are yellow   would you forgive
        me and get up
no sooner than the lake no
sooner than

TO FORM AN ADHERENT

4

But one of you stay behind
    as a spy   because I feel more alive
        than dead   appealing as my
hide pronounces   the word
    where a bear is staying inside
and I'm beaten again
    Oh   why do I range in
        this dust spring   as you always going away
in the open
drop back while the Spring burns. . . . . So fresh!

PROTECTIVE COATING WHICH INHIBITS

5

Nothing has brought me back unwilling
      O   of summer
in where a pain reserves you
unripe. I choose between the excuse
    And the shocks   that pause.
When will I come here again?
When the bee makes his house larger!
When the strings let the sun alone!

Only the spring has wings. No!

FURTHER DETERIORATION OF

6

Light! light from sugar. Light
of foam accomplishing and vanish loosely
into the changed,
awake in − − − − − −
    O flower of water's vent!

Do trees repress the long birth
they lean on? Do you
bring me to my ears?
When will I
decline with the lazy starve?
into moonlight where there's no light

THE METAL

7

Fish, what is it like?
so let me play.
How can I
push the breeze
into the murmur of fathers?
Small and white love to flowers
not being told your
crooked bite receives me, too tame

O fish,   Am I
the bumblebee in the sun's cause?

PASSION FOR THE SKY

You are near me. The night
is rectilinear and light
in the new lipstick
on your mouth and on the colored
flowers. The irises are blue.
As far as I look we are across. A
boat crosses by. There is no monkey in me
left: sleep. There is something
sold, lemons. Corn is whizzing from the
ground. You are sleeping
and day starts its lipstick.
Where do we go from here?
Blue irises.

PREGNANT, I COME

I come to you
with the semen
and the babies:
ropes of the born.

I rise up as you go up
in your consciousness.
Are you unhappy
in the source?

The clouds sputter
across the ring.
Do the birds sing?

Is the baby singing in you? yet.

SPRING IN THIS WORLD OF POOR MUTTS

I kiss your lips
on a grain: the forest,

the fifth, how many do
you want on here?
This is the same you
I kiss, you hear
me, you help:

I'm thirty years old.
I want to think in summer now.
Here it goes, here it's summer

(A disintegrated robot)
over us.
We are mortal. We ride
the merry-go-round. A drummer like
this is together.
Let's go feel the water.
            Here it goes!

Again and it's morning "boom"
            autumn
"boom" autumn
and the corn is sleeping.
It is sleeping and sweating
and draws the beautiful
soft green sky.

Walk home with the
animal on my shoulder

in the river, the river gets
deeper , the Esso gets
deeper; morning,
        morning,
        cigarette,
family and animal
and parents along the river.
Oh imagination. That's how I need you.

A flying duck or an antler refrains.
The small deer at the
animal farm walks up
to us.

A waterbug comes into
the bathroom.
The north sky is all frozen over
like a river.
Like a pimple a waterbug
comes into us
and our lives are full
of rivers. Heavy waterbug!

This is the robot and he
continues across the street.
Looking at a bird
his penis is hanging down;
a wind for
its emotions.
    I don't want to sleep.
The cold around my arms.
Like an iron lung.
As sleep comes closer to the robot's
emotion. Iron.

Spring. Spring. Spring. . . . . .
        Spring!
Spring down! come down!
There it goes! there it goes!
Arm belly strike.
Press friend push.
Teeth cruel arrow. I cannot
do without,
without do I cannot, Spring.

Chrome gladly press.
Between me, my wings. Listen as
the fireflies organize.
O save me, this Spring, please!
Before I hurt her
      I hurt her only life
      too much
and it carries in this
iron bug crawling all around.
      Is this Spring?
and it carries me,
iron bug, through the Spring.

DATA

To indicate is to
turn off   in a world
away from ease.
Rotating in a mean format of oxygen.
First make and then
made all alone until
the end of a blank.
The smoke opens up and out
comes a word
in a new storage of love.
Turning off or
turning on the calcareous bases
we find our selves in
are set there by IT.
Divine and more
divine each day, no control,
but in another world.

A SONG OF AUTUMN

A dog disappears
across a small lake.
It waits for me.
It goes where I want to go.
Begins to wake up the flowers.
So leave us alone.
Because no freedom can choose
between faces and
hours as destroyed as moving,
or cold water in the
sun. I can go out
now and measure
the flies that swing around trees
like doctors around a woman
full of bars and beauties
you could never make free;
Not even if the
flowers turn to moss and
loose sensations for their stems.

AUTUMN BREAK

For who can human back?
The race, the lameness: the divine is negro,
it's white. The indian jumps from the
ridge onto the horse.
    What things are not too near us?
I see him walking away
with you, and
    the leaves keep falling
       from the trees.

I LIKE TO COLLAPSE

   Saturday night   I buy a soda
Someone's hand opens   I hold it
It begins to rain
Avenue A   is near the river

DOWN

The rain falls
down down and jumps
jumps in my eye
as everyone I know is sleeping

by the heaviest drops.

AUTUMN-TIME, WIND AND THE PLANET PLUTO

Like a spear afterwards
        cut out,
head and eye hurts "When is he
coming to   wear me because I
    am a prisoner
full of victims
and human" she said

He was the only one with
      a skin disease.
    Tied to, he fell "I love him"   She fell
     like a stone on a rope
and instead   death instead   of arms free

    Sun testicles next
       of splashes

SOUL IN MIGRATION

How many sights
do I have that I'm
        against?
    A body and even the blesses are
a nuisance of man's
            glory. It is transitory;
a bird to
his mathematics and
song memory. My song's
had enough. My song is
enough plow courage;
again my soda is loud and
cares like a stable horse
out of a thunderbolt.
We're crazy men.

Out of a she
        I come to
you, shot or clubbed like
a fisherman without a fish.
Without a desperation to sing.
I want to be a servant
even though I try,
but this is backed
up for man's life, backed up.

Are these the high schools
        in our drinks?
To take us
        in a school of fish

oh the sea, sea

we feel

Ah like a fish.

And we could be born
irrevocable, testament, poverty,

in the garden: Then
only then will
I hear my son
change toys
at the beginning of a new day:
a wave,
a splash.

DRUNKEN WINTER

Oak oak! like like
it then
   cold some wild paddle
so sky then;
flea you say
"geese geese" the boy
June of winter
of again
Oak sky

WILD PROVOKE OF THE ENDURANCE SKY

Be uncovered!
Hoe with look life!   Sun rises.
Rice of suffering. Dawn
        in mud,
this is roof   my friend
O country   o cotton   drag
of the wild provoke,
there's a thousand years   How are
you growing?
No better to in a stranger.
Shack, village,
                brother,
wild provoke of the endurance sky!

STRUGGLING

We are going   the park.
There are swings.
There are rocks   a sand bed.
The flowers rest
the bed. The flowers
rise. We are fatigued
but invade them.
There is a smell.
It invades us.
It hides us.
Notice! there are flowers along
the bed, tiny flower clusters.
But we cannot move our legs.
We cannot move our eyes.

GROW

I fight and fight.
I wake up.
The oasis is now dark.
I cannot hear anything.

The wind is felt
and the stars and the sand
so that no one
will be taken by pain.

I sit next to the bushes,
Hercules couldn't move me,
and sleep and dream.

The sand, the stars are solid
in this sleeping oasis,
alone with the desert and
the metaphysical cigarette.

DANGERS OF THE JOURNEY TO THE HAPPY LAND

Talk of energy.   Mayan sub-flower
Come to light and feel physically intent to
plasm
    Even if I don't share
    Instance the mother
Talk of energy or stolen from her
mother
    I didn't do that for
nothing   I speak as a wife to the
capsizing Both are once
Perspire like an autumn wind bakes. Mayan
sub-flowers.
    Am I allowed to go to
the tough section? That's tough.
    Mayan sub-flowers in
        the shade.

RISK

It is made up of (in our latitude)
wind through an inflamed solar plexus.
The lobelias are so close to
the offbeat.
O candy for our sore,
        Lend to beggars   the
hound, the flowers in season,
the Rough Sun
        sun of the ripened
nearly concocted colder than night
            O summer

HAPPINESS IN THE TREES

O height dispersed and head
in sometimes joining
these sleeps. O primitive touch
between fingers and dawn
on the back

You are no more
simple than a cedar tree
whose children change
the interesting earth
and promise to shake her
before the wind blows
        away from you
in the velocity of rest

FLY

The lights are on;
flesh is next to the body.
Drinking out of the glass
and the tide sways
you in my arms.
A membrane of wisdom
or the lips. I spit.
Nothing is changed.
The lights are on.
The sound of the waves
        through the traffic. I rub your body.
Hold me: the waves.
A fly alights
        on the glass.
It sings a song
with a nerve impulse.
And the tide
        noticed by
the birds———— fit to eat
comes back in
the dream of a metropolis.
The flies full of
energy, full of light   alight.

THE BOOK OF WILD FLOWERS

I can't live blossoming drunk
this story of climbed up
Be world to   any apples!
be anxiously! Hurrah
the desert   Ream them! Feed them!
I can't live blossoming drunk
                   oh
chicory sun (to daughters)   dawn
to the yellow stings
to lean   frim fram   up
on   so I knoll   rushing rush-
ing   against . . . . oh hum of dawn
against the knoll

IN MY CRIB

I

    Autumn is very   wild though
not like   you   You hear
autumn is
         coming O seasons
Are you like the crib?
Can I understand what I
don't like?   Loneliness is my crib.

The limeland is   not the
         honesty I need

2

Why do we have to
work, fluttering liveliness? I am not
sick. He's looking at me.
Space is between us
fluttering liveliness

3

Autumn is very sad
though not   like you. You
hear autumn   is
coming   O seasons
Are you the crib?   Can I
understand what I
like?   I am sitting
   in my house.

DON'T BREAK IT

He played with a toy   they bought
candy   She played with a toy
Do not be afraid of the bear
They placed their arms around the bear
Around them the sea
listened but didn't talk   because it
can't talk, neither can stars
which emit for no one   The gods
can't hear because they are not any place
      Friendly the bear embraced them
back.   The zoo is a nice
place to live, you are caged in the zoo
In the zoo is the world. Everyone
chews at a different rate and
stars do not emit
I am waiting for you at the
north entrance
          into the zoo
Going back we looked at the few
plastic clouds into the dark moony
trees

SPRING

All I will amount to: knowing
your sound, small bees,
the winter wind
is green.

BOOK III from *FITS OF DAWN*

The green lake is awake

O gong of wept

O unviolet
    furious cozy the rain
O dam of soul

to chase look! am poor.
    dimanche poor.

O cheat of beg   o cat
gist o am   Walk

elysium tool a sun day   Broke
revel lasso to
Yes, wolf of songs, O muse
O mixed Enemy!   Invent

of dwell   So voyage   So end mercy
earth   Usurp violets

O visible gym of flowered

Partly in skies in weak muzzles, fertile
   communal dodging america.
Unwhorl sagesse pain!
Am finally teen so
morning that chime the running   The
Fun   Stop morning full rubber
of mountain to shun for
our active milk elope   The
Bottom

Am bottom am summer, am
there, hero   Seed allegheny hum verge
beckon teen unquick
unquick pieds couteau egress above

Defend, I ate song fins,
Am gush some bang of ode
conjure you must
I food and swim. . . . .
equal torture you personal
you wing soon
        Violent dishing my rush
stung of sorry   Themselves themselves
Tool soon fathom-seer-to-doze
theodosia to sonnet
drifted sono upthing, volcano reads.   Saviour
famish it is moves.
Catalyst so june so admit
Ranch! Ranching that votre like
misery prosody somnambula
being going being crime.

futile ment
at stroll for to
gulp
               On rain joint
               ill a shuffle
               little though
               trees got

Stem   feign to love
non flowers a   Tent as shoot
way so
nod of   apples dizzy

Terrible over!
Tent will boy?
Myself stroll final ment
at shuffle for to
gulp

               Why see!
               terre yes the
               save
               temp cistern
               for sorry
                    pawn
               oh sunday yes
               system of
               supine from milk
               neant so sly
               for sorry

Lotus non off
room bereave for
supine of sunday   "oh
fist je tout"
Communal all the
spare Trust! Ster-
ile! a reedy fuss de-
spair

Toy for the raking gully
shame encore there,
sorry human posed working,
demeanor just helen as
garden comes, Music
o cotton unforgiven bargain,
chilly, gush, album in later manjun
embrace.   Begs soon jamais
furious bungalow of
pour a boy.   Scowl possess however
city trumped,
jumbles pity then, rum or
canto sleep in this eddy.
To a rumble Hour lo a grape
sleep   please graphic
to ours like ate
quivers place then float
came came wack ill of voices
god of
    Picnic lumin and
sake in Talk! Sort!
dose Ah slave and
premate Correo to
until of mades, asylum budding,
possessed sop churning,
woman tippling wings hill.
Young over ahoy
for the breathe

O targets! and sang   O timid of
among!   Off! Saying!
yellow shook then Pan! O

Completely leaf.
Yet prize!
alone aesop damage

Night for the carnival
rummage of humans

O outside O nervous yellow
silo for the harm
          And soul
Really game smother nowhere
summit   Yes
    oar kill happen of enamoured

                    Jungle
for my surely quake
smallen smallen stung of surged
    The birth
            Rampart! Bat! Perhaps!
    The drink   the whistle

there maybe
of the down
Not pine   Not scowl
prolific binge to wane,
orchard gyp afraid of
conch of frolick! Yes,
no fist, the soon trestle trestle fake So
malheure a shy for bunch

                    "poseidon"
                        Donné
        Farmest ecoutez o meadow
                    of pay

        O shine of
            could
                Bark!
            Rooster for muffle
                    Killed
        O seem

                    begin poor
                serious Demeter   O
        hilly erg of
                                young
                being of otter being
                    apollo
        O Voyez! O whelm
                        Succumb
                painty of dommage
            Bloom! O tox
                destroy N
                    oregon of motion

                Lore curious of milk
                O body   spill
                    degree enfance
                                cane of
        oaxaca. Today
                force infant
            flowerous than earth

Only the wand
        openly la playa
        la plage
                        told
    winter aesop,

behind october worse, worse than belts
    of caracas then
        mind   O hunger   Livid
            swish

                        bullet
    remind a reed o
        gravel connaitre
                        wack to doze

Dreamt of cheat
                    cheat of
            suddenly soul dawn ocean
    lasso for the
                Jealous!

Only violent elysium of
                    the jetty
            saving ploughs   O
        lotus   O coon
                that grain
    . . . . . . O
        breathe

A STORY FROM THE BUSHMEN

"Are you an eland?"   Yes! Yes!
She ran off to the primeval forest
and there gave birth to an eland
Her husband holding the calf to his
chest ran to the hills: placed
the beautiful child in a fault
which was surrounded by other faults
among the hills /
While the child grew, he (the husband)
created all the animals and
ways in which the animals were to
be caught; and also the wind which
was to follow the animals
being hunted
Their child, the eland, had grown horns
and only the sun was more
beautiful than he   But other
sons of the father of the eland crossed
the little calf in his sleep
and killed it because it was more
beautiful than anything they had ever seen.
Their father who had created
all animals tore off the noses of his
sons who had killed without
knowing what they had killed. But later
saying "No I won't do this,"
put their noses back on
        The wife cleaned her pots and
put the blood from her dead
eland son mixed with the fat from

its heart: and stirred, stirred
then sprinkling it about, each drop
became an eland which
ran into the woman with his horns
 See! you have ruined the
  eland: and thousands were made
    And the father ordered the
sons to hunt the elands and to
see whether they could kill one
But Cagn, the father was
in the elands: and none
could be killed:
because they were even faster
than any cloud

sonne bell Sonne guilt like the
unrosed stark Ecstasy gen
d'alume no world
disbanishment unlook See! See!
     occident am the sky
To cistern insist we lie
Swim, World!
deja everything already
and see

Peaks grand the fruit soleil o
 turbule wept for lily
  oh see That nights
Border irrelevant sweet for wounds
  like the careful orion and
   blooms

Is the sky husk moldy
unison newal o please?
Sickle mads pro other weak
reef annoy mew
among o sway tones musing at
Lo lo dull off the forest,
moon frozen. Emptier that

shook. Oh upon
          of songs   Breathe!

grateful soccer monet churning oh savage
of must   Overboard! small laquel embraced
Once are the alley easily
of supine   once
stood!   bad!
suffer and village!

    O scarcely
verge o stings   Where is a new
        beg of morning matin?
                "yes" of the hand?

delve sky against   Nude
mandarin d'etoile
A tour of slept Slept!: the pacific
    the vine of orange of
              sommeil

Mads of dawn! Rape of you you. . . .
    o the autumn sand

Mounting!
   O dive!
song song restay fairness of
dawn. That cry of
booze that sparrow
of soul "miradel"
unique justly lotus
nothingless char of sunday.
Vicious of moon for the actual.
Live digress

Old like the praise cast
still at day   Assuage
of rose of eye
lovingly sun
   O sun with the dreadful
of kind   Man! full! of the organ
               of move
Shoulder are the vines
are the plus are the
autumn of found are the fallen
blank are the aussi
     the loping soon
        the wet

blank the soleil les fleurs
the Force of rainbow
   shout the fishing
quell quell.   River of sacred
         pitifully fairly

   admiring cane from
        cane one enemy sings
to find to
      bird oh
   ladle of fix
     oh severally plund of
cruel, like mars
    for my earth,
like loom for the understand.

To need am the fly
The breathe no pavillion to this
pain.   Nape, so
the precipice is june   But for the
villanous level joyful
as the town so play

Spring & Summer 1961

WATER: HOW WEATHER FEELS
THE COTTON HOTELS

I

The woodwind light
rollever breast sounds
a misnomer   travel on
tracks of
weather   sufficient
explanation cours
the river blank

          mask mean bundle
             entrails

    I shall saw
    wood saw I
    see the beach of windy feet
        so feel
    wool had grown on
    last sweater until
    he had heard

summer
the terrace people tomorrow
    Who has opened (generously)
        the well?
dispersion the expressed height
from over
a sea person
young fifteen year old
      algebraic breeze upon
      the curtain (hangs)

exit   enter low
     tide
the gang sponge
vase sounds of
what corn breathes ?
is under commission   a
juniper
             of take left before
          the valley skates
            the shadow hawk
   what great decisions   who
licks the young chest (breast) ?

2

   A small listen perched
left in the wait of those
impoverished he s
Some highland march grass
       tree here   maybe there
       to roll the
       sharp gardens on   thighs
       grow tied to
       the climate of here
Space
mathematical hybrid
is nature alone ?
representative to
     and green with longing
An attempt has
   failed (cards
in a coop of grass)
investigate ! it is

necessary to cross
                        eruption blocks
below
     the marker sand
     Shall I wire night besides
     great exposition
     certain words under which
     I step out into
               sudden sun in summer
               clearest frost december

     unwrap the weather for
     it's grown old
     and you in
     at home speedily by the something
     but then to bother with
     the secret
     the forms in most critical
                    position
     followed by
               Oh lucky slide
          the backyard of where
                    no trials   as when
                    and by long window
               silence
     we learned

3

     one distinction of the clouds
     Again you are young busy
               the leaves
               of human predicate

forget and thought of summer
by disappointment
where

    1 bed is to share
    with twelve others
    11 children (more or less)
    1 or 2 wives
    come in !

within balcony fiords
you act strangely
sweating (sweet) some anatomy   who
has prepared bread
and goldfish for the rooms ?
my eyes have endured (shuddered)
the affection of hands

please this being not enough
    show me
the cotton gear (queer)
    of death
we should all die men
we should all die women

Who is it ? runs through
    marsh voices damp
        from dew

if night would pass over
    me like a ship
        in my twist
beneath the sleep

this cat the master
counts years in whiskers
　　of this cat
　　　　　　　remain flexible
　　　　　provisionally let me go
　　　　　　for end

4

but unlike Le metro
percussion　turns
where can you river
　　　object waves the plainest
　　　　blue horizon
　　　　to contact the recurring
　　　　　crowds
　　　　chop up all the
　　　　　　　　momentary
　　　chatter and the clouds
　　　　See we are all
　　　　great behind
　　　us the sound we walked
　　　night

　　　dromedary summations

yes we know the
　　lip wanings
of the waves against
　　your breast

　　　　and here it is mid
　　　　december the

                sky
                        still blue

and this river that has
Calm!   the january branches
Slope sun
            declining
journeys trace about
the factory towers having
given up their form
to the atmosphere blue
        and purplish a
        faded banner of surface

passing through this
            plain relief

the river. . . . . .

            this moment
            my strength hangs
            small festoons on
            this cliff and its
            corollary of trees

We could not touch eas-
        ier this confused design
        in the birds that
            gather weeds
        assume and designate
        small windy gathering
        of wood
certain limpness
            forgotten

5

      . . . . . . turbine
we cannot forget the
      condensation
of the mornings
between the 18 seconds
               the ride
increasing twins elevating
living by what we
would rather
      leap

the windy shelf

I suppose that you would rather live
through all this
the light the moon on
    earthenware
drawing its own
tonight on some
particular wasp

and you are only 18
     in the only
  kind

so we are states and
     not a word the
     mellow stillness
     of the sounds are
     still

Things come down in adequate bundles
to the crow

who speaks ?   dress warmly !
to the bell from which
it is part

                    things defounded
Marcel clambered rocks in hat
and everything apart
from breeze of
highway moving downways
Pass the reticent principle stem
        interrupt vocality !

San Juan Teotihuacan
the mud branches of your pyramids
now in New York and
        branches like this november
the sun and cactus
    of your fruit
the orange season

6

Taking bread from his scratchings he
grew and in the thickest theater
remained a spectacle an ornament
of forgetfulness where nothing comes
back and nothing came from but the
small impediments like starch on
humming birds' wings.

7

            I had told you of
                the storm in full

of red children
which we perceive of
how to man the machine
surely lose our valley
                    disposition
well (water) has African wind
                    women

always good for any
real moment life
is already covered with
contact the subject swim
he is a good
        valley food growing
        young again tired buttocks
        spoke the fox soldiers

Subject breeze that
finds your way bridge
the appler stretching the
disappointed that you could not

mischief food
        I've grown the last descent

outside——the poor balloons
   luck elbow   why come ?
      havana ! havana !

who speak travels ?   I
see you alone obtain
        afternoon's pronunciation
I also know it
the armadilla acts the car

                    waiting
            desert tunes the fan

                Turn where light performs
            his own composition for
                    saxophone now ruminates
            some tan notes
                    cool brown
                    snow (saxophone)
                    falling
                    on my toe

        Last time we fumbled
        What time are animals ?
        Walk   oh
                        overlooking

8

        Then there is nothing   think !
        the angular explanation
        boom !   he was a parade
                    with a gift
        a question cable of
                        thought
        a thermos savage in
                    the hotel
        in vera cruz color
                .   sand the boat !

        the ship weighs on the
        east   Bobbing
        in sea

                    she burns us
at the turn
    her eyes turn like the
        motion of a ship

Let the careful prolific
shade or else the
falsity of summer in the dry
a motion holding
the blankest
        wish my hand

Come out !   because
        I fall into spring (primavera)
a proof that every
        is the first seeing
        the path is like the
            few leaves on the top step
turned by the
        opening of
        the door (swiftly)

    it had been almost
            months and each its
                first step
    like a distance between
            their smiles   were
    hurry channels
    contrasting the wood snow

        Ho !   river
walk softly for instance
        in park talk
that evening had no
    wish to go

When we had come to the exact center it was
there we should have to complete the last dash
realizing we had made a new arrangement through
which——could look at our sun pass through
entanglements. It was at this point I walked
down to people below——moving slightly (the air).

                  for when have we not
                                    desirable ?

9

    Print open me   the
    car goods awake are drowning
        in the wake water
    leave behind
            sleeping and brought to
            a condoning dawn

    the full chief and singing
    enter !   someone like a couple
                the country fermenting
                the hill's edge and
        middle green with lipping
            there are   the old
                        sake

                    constantly near my entire
        years   stumbled in———
    feet dirty

    and you come forward
            from switzerland

what I shall never
    be able to answer
walk over me I
    feel   what earth

CONTRAST

It's here in whatever shoots come up.
There's not a sound.
Like blossoms and grasshoppers
under the snow breathing little holes.
Is it death trying to see and breathe?
But I can't ask you to go.
       Do you understand?
What do you see?
The white snow,
the grey spears, oh grasshoppers,
       you rough grasshoppers
that are deader than a grasshopper
against my raw heart.

FLOATING GARDENS

Sailing Sailing
under the creatura ridge,
and this less or more than obscure,
obsequious life follows the lives
of flies on beach.
"I'm happy," I said to big tree.

So we stand
on a ridge, it
has corners and we
wait in corners
of excellent summer,
unconscious manifolded igneous
summer,
and the flies on the pillow, sheet,
and cactus colored window
buzz the chandelier great white weather.
I'm far from a window.
Yet I am window and
feel the multicolored pushes
through open window self .

O HEART UNCOVERED

We lived in province snow range
and something that we uncover
is like living
in one Arizona room
when we discover all we owe
to darkness
we never really know.

Tomorrow is the national holiday for independence—
no more left.
For the first time
we see the mountains
with snow on them pulling away
from the mountains and clouds.

PAIN SONGS

Back; gone country around,
like wind in hollow rabbit.
How many steps to take to
mud around, across,
Ixtapalapa green canal?
The cow is green, the
flax is brown; brown life
of flies, cool color, sickness, eyes.
Many over, what then?
There Jose stumbled on
market stands, dogs bit my clumsy foot.

Transport the ground, and
trees of olives like mouth
of understanding boulevards,
of green light mountains
where hills are filled with
lizards' feet near home.
A silence as white as hospital clouds.

O breeze,
when I was young
and tried hard, when I was
there among 1000 footers,
off on off on the bird
on in, gone in in in flew.
Alone. The straw's
alone, the grave's alone,
the twitch, the switch,
the bitch's alone,
above clouds higher than moods.

It's late and the air's
as thin as straw,
and hill droves of relativity,
of hornet's hair sleep cool
as a quiet nosey rat.

Climbing up we passed it by,
maybe it was the cactus on
the knee or lizard in his pee.
It looked straight up as sun
boomed in rocks and big
zapilote bird made a shadow.

They asked me,
You going where in leaves?
Going when in road?
Sitting with all this sidewalk similarity.
It's like a bed unfolding
some high transportation of the street.
It is too much for street
here. How high it seems.

Pain, like blue is the
strap of night, the goulash
of darkness, a pool
of energy and green light signs;
signs of red, signs of night.
I leave, sandals fastened:
breeze warm as my hands, warm
as these warrior's hands.
I refuse, but accept that
if nothing else, there's
breath as thin as paper.

The path, the path is where?
It's the cow's, o but
to be near the cow.
Let's be near some old
realization that just died.
Near some depowdered
head that comes around
the horseshoe curves of sense.

But I discovered along the hedge
of waking that this
is me,
and around my skinniness I
place my clothes of disinterest,
and I bathe it, and
I bathe me anonymous.
I am unknown.
And in a rail-
road yard at dawn.

Biting a stick wondering
what it's all about under
the orange tree gloom bridge.
Let's count and
amount to everything we're
not supposed to.
That talk is from a young
brain, in a rebitten valley
of feathers, sky, beach,
sea, bush, volcano hump in the distance.

It's the sand perverse on
the boulevards that
swim Veracruzian desolation

in deep vocabulary afternoon:
a knot of sun commingles
the cactus, the sea, the plateau.

The day turns over on its
spine. Every faucet's
on. Ah! in the
haze, the grip running wall,
the sun grouping on the stillness
of your dark tide.
What sea gull blindness
on rocks, dunes, oil
pumps of your thoughts.
And the builders rinse their mouths and
the days of a week go swimming away.

There is a creek that passes.
It's a creek that
travels and looks like a bone,
within which all memory itself
has been.
There's no memory outside this.
There is only it.
I want the creek,
the feeling of its
depth like a body
on the fingers.

The morning awakes
and leaves me with one
hard thing. The summer
months sit on
a steeple (the only one around),
and the magnifying glass

of occupations leaves
the doors of a monsoon open,
growing from ridges of your lips.
You are young,
all roofs of world cannot
crush the highways of your newness.
When you're gone
it's as if someone
has taken away
the steps to a temple.

Wind is warm in the
store windows. It's November.
Surprise ducks leave a
canopy of a lake over the avenue.
To keep these secrets
we allay the nobody
seen on the cheeks of everyday.
Here! wear this spirit insignia.
Don't ask.
The line grows from yesterday.

Tomorrow it rained.
The light is mattress lipped,
and the pages born curtains.
Here! bang on my hand
frozen since Montezuma.
"Los pajaros," not yet.
Whistle my breath
to the banging hammer hotel
and the Indian yellow blouse baby
carrying dirty serape beauty.
I listen
as I eat the street for supper,
listen to the pain songs

of Mexico.
Flashes of returning
come with the birds.

MIGRATORY NOON

        Cold and the cranes.
Cranes in the
                wind
like cellophane tape
on a school book.
The wind bangs
the car, but I sing out loud,
                help, help
as sky gets white
        and whiter and whiter and whiter.
Where are you
        in the reincarnate
                blossoms of the cold?

CHAINS OF MOUNTAINS

The clouds are panting.
There is a subequal brightness.
It makes my eyelids shake
in the morning submarine of leaves.
I think: where would my
dog be if I had one?
Like this brightness that's rubbed
in the morning.
And I touch this piece
            of metal and it is cool
cool as a morning swim.
But I hear no mountains.

NOTE FROM ST. FRANCIS

In the world today
there is
no world so attached as I am
to worlds.
All our hairyness
all our coarseness.
There is no texture in this
warmth I feel about
the creatures today.
We are gunning for extinction.
The sky is still bright
and all the animals running
for prehistoric sounds
believable in the passionate night.

CROSS FIRE

This is the second day without anyone.
I am chinning against a dark sky
to strengthen my arms.
A picture of everyone I love passes thru me.

No clear light streams thru this cell.
There's no dawn.
What have I gained
by lying in this abyss,
waiting for the masonry
to show a little slit
for my soul to get through?

FIRE OF MYSELF

What I miss most is
          that live
that subtle transformation
     from inert to
trans-atomic structures
that leaves my welded
and supple body
that carries the imprint
          of that body
into the land
     of pure migration

STAR SONG

December!   end!
this
beneath my house
alongside
by
into
of milk silver
that sprang up
in
leaves which
         bloom
and as
in the. . . . .

O stars!

SEA LEVEL

Open to me, my sister, my love, my dove, my undefiled, for my head is full of dew, and my locks of the drops of the night. —The Bible

PART I

Bush

       She is not wearing
shoes or a dress   I begin to change.
Breath will pass like the breeze
it is   I am
    changing   Swimming
       in a wave

I'm walking over here. I'm not
like a prisoner.   Don't
bother him, flies toward   the cells
   Spread their cells. There's free
misery in the cell
       How does
this cheap kiss
(walking over) find the real you
         and your cells?

What's the name of this
   sea level?   I can't
get up   It's so   diligent to
shine   The shoes are   not shining
in the kitchen
       The birds are twirping
in the bricks   They are burnt siena

What gives you a
    shot towards the
      island?

Where is your name on this
island?   To come here
without knowing   anyone at all
What courage in
the absconding night.   "Running

      but to disconnect"

I try to sleep but I
can't know. She is

    sleeping   She isn't
old   She seems like
a stranger but I
    can't know

cooling the first
    headaches

    Night is never

a stranger of
    terrible pain   In the clown of depths it can't know
timing delicate blood,

    tigers through her
    shining, a stranger
      of   delicate children purging

in the bay   beside
    who he wants to sleep

I can't know what it is to lie there and dead because if I'm a passerby and adjoining the luscious surrounded smiles, I could say I was dishonest. If he could be arab maybe I could learn something about dreaming or the lungs; what bite at the intestine when there's such a long way to go down through them into the field. I can't snicker because I know my controls peeking at all the people evaluates me and changes and dependent over a veiny sea, that I love to swim in. But am afraid of the nutrition of this lust. It doesn't look like a life. But I know it is.

Never deserted, even if the desert is gas.

What is my
  wife's hardship
at random happening
in the fallen middle of day
Does she find Weak?
but the grass is
hidden in deep grass. Pikes do not
grow thin One breast

 The light's coming in through
the glass on the door
 The night outside is
not troublesome or
 manes of night
  belonging. Through the dating
shrunk air the light's coming in through
the glass on the door

      Where did
you go? O summer long
 air How's the city
Take off your shirt!
  Here is my skirt, she said.

When the native sets
over the wall, I grieve
to be honest real.
         Why should?   filled with
the monkeys   I play   with you

By the time to return
no head sees. O to have my breast see in
tawdry, my breast
seen in the simplest
     life around   The complicated
         ah me or ma
shushed in the leaden band of a look
     Shame can never go
with kites, the will light opening
     opens beyond you

Mouth lined in masses

Be the other   one! You
no die   Where there
     is rest by poor

That as of an ape
     of this. Us in you. You no
     be my ape, he said.

and took off on the path.

     How do we man it
in the time in
     the matter do we love or do
we make it   how do
we man it?

Flowers grow in Tancredi and
mexicans we turn in
bellows of sons

A place when some violet one string genital meets a flower
The flower says I like the noise in the streets And through the
noisy fence I cry "why don't you use it" Growing in the light at
the backs of flowers atune like a vigilante kid feeling he can't
find his horse; There is the sun

I'm with you to see
        the bear   Are they the bear?
Or it is this with another.
        Plain of the west.   Mother you be
in or as if all
ridges and girls do.   Go
                on the plain!
        We are in or woe.

In the yellow bright salt
west all are without no
        besiege,

        In winter the yo yo to
pity, the tight drinking
        opposite the yo yo

                gives the rain and safety
        new fissure in our blood
in the winter.
        We are tying
        How are we tying? the ka ka to
the shore to the boy.

I'm not complete yet to go out with a light face in the shade
or the drinks that turn to our hideouts. Into the cutting waves
I wind an eagle to our legs and go a thousand miles to the table
to eat. We don't even think of softness or the shy lakes in the
woods turning to friends, we shine from "benign I have drunk"
between us. He met her, there wasn't anything there until he
prepared for sleep; then their whole object came back and that
part of their heads.

Now you ask me how old! I'll need a native and why should
I ask for war with you, or the herida pain of peace or strangers.
She comes to him by the car and all colors fade. He is surprised.
To the girl on her feet the boy's leg loses its curve.

    O shepherd of
the eskimos watching the white
innoculated sheep, where is
the river of cuntelating light, where is
the Passaic or Nile?
    (on this map) o mommy (the kid
said) wake me up; this
mass is its own light.

PART 2

Incense

The north that we made holds my gel
that has love sitting there
month and the unmonth.
Where are the moving gels? What do
the moms do to us?
Where is the tomb of my
passion as a man
Flexed so that unity says to me, "The air
for the group, woman, pains, and
man cool of another liver"

has this in me all to the fragrance
of orbits. Fragrant,
as the first path of a bee.

(There's so many rows of flowers and
rabbits return to accompany
their caresses. There are
no caverns to their hair.
Over wavey and cool kisses,
signs revert to us.
The mane falls asleep.)

Ask you o curable separate
internal, of what the
answer and revolt was to go. Even if we
loved reinternal and went
for the seed and shared.
He had it no better. But he had it
for advent. Is this how we fly with
an ancient? It is. What furious
orders "to be next."
To be part of that which says
"He doesn't fake it"   Where are you trying?
Of the want is low.
And when by my own am
    I in hock to
    see you? To record
you with no addition by
    the up and remade?
The pose and "in" is an
enemy or should he
froth the ins?
What furious
orders "to be next."

O sunsuit, blue sunsuit
of children in the
lead and Euphrate sun

"That's called the tree"
Put together what he wants. What
do you want?
    Because she's a mind a
hoop: like a river.
      A girl is to hold
       a beast. As other himself.
Grow absorbed as one beast is
         to the passion of different knowing.
        Hold its body
      as he crosses the street.

      I want to enhance you, but I'm as
perishable as october fruit in the brown
ripe flower going to bed.
        Go to sleep Pauly!
             The leaves are spreading and
             decoying for you
             Because it's
             quiet in its
             imperishable decoy. The rope
             of love and feathers   vining to
             you   o   misery   o
             first attains of flight
The man sits in the Lord
In the each, woe.
What in them each, bright
as the sunrise in them each, to oppose
as the day so rises west, opposite
high love in dust tin, and

sees the crow at
world practising inside.

But no he had it for him
Add and comes it
The pale are right
Has he the pale friend?
To whom do you allay?
To the seed of Marylyn?
The cat fakes the
dog, a mamma or a
foe.
How we are your poor.
What did they say to you?
How we yearn

Why, conjugal fire
don't you send down, cut short a
figure to belong to myself and humans,
personify me?   a present
that's a disappointment of human
teams; like the eagles
in the next level.

Oh desire, be conjugal when
you send down the simple
fire flys; like regulators of a
new planet; calculate and redeem
me into more earth, oh
primordial bug, into bug, painless
and unpopular, pregnable and
                    light-weight.

Sag wherever. You went by this heart,
stern, holding on, raining and disturbed.
Bald is the disturbed train
that holds a mirage;
     Plants and more than
     beginning mint;
Than who is that feel.
Indeed free from change.
Sit on my knee from change.
Completed his enjoyment of white, stripes
of black males
Unborn is resin.
One sits and eats, the other watches
Complete interest in the
other.   Then the many feet
       Bliss sheltered.
A black fruit like the dawn. See
          from itself!
"It's that all right"
The packs   And full   oblation

This film is like the butter itself. This tent
is like the ant in water.
Does youth go out of a man like the happy ants go out
of a dead man? The discovery that
forebears proposition to speak, and
images to cut short the hex
seasons. From
consume or knowledge,
  o beautiful,
than its will to speak. Where can we
corner you? as the afternoon
rises like a sheep's ba?
Is it only souls that can become
resplendent?

How I peace.
Let me know when.
You can other me in a trillion different ways;
It finally shears
the bad night. You are without legs.
Are you leaving me flat? How
are you going to kiss,
if someone has your nature?

You could never finish with
someone you have spoken.
Coming essence adorns
the poor rages of honesty inflamed
as rice in your heart:
love pitted and rising in your
arm, thieves holding a season, placenta,
and miracles of balms
constructed of what you are o
drill; under this drought
beholding, the thief of living with you,
of living with you.

Come to me under me! venus is
not second in this gloss

"My labor tremors when I think of
being inside you, my loss.
Then why don't I just tell you
about the hoodlum of my nil;
leopard and banging kissing to be yours.

GRASS

What good is it comprising myself
softly as the bemused colored fish?
Do I think I'm the beautiful pants?
What a desolate street!
Why are the swamp weeds
tickling me
How could I be killed
if I'm the duck who wipes away
the dark holes made
by bullets as I continually displace
energy, pulling through snowing clouds?

ROUTE

There were more dirty
   things   They were dirty
Our hair was
long and blind   To eat

Diner is very
   crowded   We have
money   Trucks are parking in
the sun
     Do not feed the
animals   We are
animals   Our cheeks are
   warm   Waitress lips   are kissing
our cheeks   Hurrah!

MAY

     I am lost.
I had swum before.
There is no deformation fatigue
         Residual under salt water
Morning oh May flower! oh
May exist. Built.
When will water stop
cooling? Built, falling. Reeds. I am surprised.
Weakness. Torsion.
The wind, white.
Sapphire, oxidation. Million. . . . . .

THE GREEN LAKE IS AWAKE

PART I

The womb can
remind you of mosquitoes
if you imagine you are
in a carriage with a net
over it

A negro is shining the
top of a used car. The pennant
is above him.

Where are you? Here I am
crossing the street. This is
my mommy. O sun!

A dog walks over to the
little boy. He walks over
sideways and bashful.
The boy throws a rock to him

The shell goes around and the
car turns over. The sunlight
is as clear as a
green bottle.

Man walking with his
shoulders haunched and tufts
of white duck hair in the back
of the head!   where were you born

The day is like splattered glass
The girls are wearing
bright sweaters and blouses.
They stop to let the cars pass

Life is green. Love is gray.
Purple are girls going to
school in wine jackets.

You stand at the corner of two
walls. Like handball
courts and a big bee
flies around you.

   There are many trees around
here. A bird flies crazily
      to one.
      Will he
      go in or not?

   A group of boys are waiting
to go in a yellow bus. A bird
down below flies over the
wall past me. Its front is blazing.

   I am walking slowly. My feet
won't move. A rheingold truck
drives past me.

   Rosemary is drinking
tea. Paul is running in his
sunsuit. The phone separates
      us. They are eternal.
            The phone is hot.

If you can imagine
a park, then you can
    see this crushed lollipop.

PART 2

I feel the cold peach
in my pocket. I am not
wearing a sweater.

    Advance as I come to
you!   Alcohol comes to us.

Open your hand; the
fly springs away. The
air is cool on this spring-
board. The water must be cool.

    Paul is watching me. His
eyes get sleepy with intensity.
He looks like he's
going to sneeze.

A whale was swimming near the coast last night.
The cement truck turns and I
realize how totally abandoned
all these workers are in their
easy happiness. But are they in
a combination of the wind?
I was looking all over for
            you.

Summer Dragon
A woman is walking. Her dress
is green as the grass and as
surprising. She has a hunched
back and her hair is
    gray like autumn grass
      and she walks
    looking down along the
grass lost and penetrating.
Is autumn

    A Song
    Why am I so dumb
now that you're gone;
now that you are gone?

The trucks behind me are
going at blasting power
A man walks toward
    me. The sun is blasting
the green shiny weeds
that are all around
        There is no one on the
        road. The road curves.
        I can't see where it goes
            The bushes move but
            the telephone pole doesn't

The roller goes over the
asphalt. The song "Love where
are you now, now that I need
you so" comes to me.
The roller goes over.

But the rain falls down
and tatters away
my balls.

The whistle blows.
    Where are you now?
People cross the street
They are all carrying something.

    What is this half feeding?
This half happiness
that hops at me
    last night?
    We picked you up last night
and you were beautiful,
the internal sunset
after the darkness
has stopped moving.
The plant that emits
a fragrance with all mothers.

In you, I feel
the new kite.
What are your feelings
                        like?

    O chemical and possible
flash,   The song goes
    on and on; the song.

PART 3

No mine is like
        the presents I want

              to give you:
         wet lips, solar aches,
roadway dust, and
the rays of the moon
at the spots where they start.
I was born
before both of you
but like a man
I'm being withered
by you both
              into the dust
         of the moon
that you have brought
         back on your feet.
I see you both
and I am dispersed
like clouds mixing
like children skating.

Working writing and
decorating this star bright
misery.   This pure
and lovely porto rican
waist.   Where do
they work?

    The little boys are fishing.
Just concentrating on hearing.
A sound of wheels squeaking
is in the trees.
Forever the sound goes on
like crickets, like night or
birds that call along
the highway and are barely
seen.

How long can I sit here?
Rest! The night is
being held by
    light droplets

    Ride your bicycle, my negro
green as the lake and
black as the trunks of trees.

I hear the train. I am
calling to the lake. "Goodbye."
    I turned my head fast.
I thought it was you at
a glance.
But it was a lady
carrying a fishing net.
She's younger than I thought.

A group of people touch
    me. What a life!
What a saw!
Charge me! oh silent
    zoo-bird.

I walk around this
leaf falling park
    Will I meet
someone I know, so far away?

Am I a Part of this
wheel of matter? just
because I am made of matter?
    I too disappear like solids;
. . . . . tomorrow night.

The green lake is awake

There are brown leaves
on the ground
    but I don't see even one
    in the full trees.

I was born a fluid.
The sun is shining on
half of the sign "Steel Pier."
    Magnifying.

    The white duck is
blue along the water.
It skates slowly
    back and forth far
from me.
            My head will be warm
            because the air is warmer
            than the water.

I will see the duck like a baby
            coming towards me.

PART 4

It is time to go
    Love me! even when I falter.
The autumn leaves are
now beginning to start
falling.

I am awake: like
a colloid

just discovered in
        a breeze.

The truck woke me up.
        Assembling outside.
Two birds fly
over the street. They are on their way to some
    food. People are
continuing into their
building, to work.
        How friendly are
        those birds to
        each other?

The bee is coming closer to me.
It is like a flying object.

The duck is bobbing up and down.
It stays almost
in the same spot
as the water under it
moves away like a river.

The leaves are falling only
when the wind blows.
I have five minutes.

How I would like to just fall
asleep . . . . in the
movement . . . . . of all this
. . . . with you
near by me as I stretch
out my arm . . . . . .
    with all these leaves
rolling across

              each other
Ditto, what suffering.
Accumulation.
Love,
degeneration, . . .
and regenerated dives

Every man or woman has
his own generator of love.

                This autumn,
                this autumn.
                    beard,
                this autumn.

The crack in the wall
goes to the left
then to the right
continues down.
It stares at me.
It stares at us.
Paul is with us, you
are with us.
The stars are uncontrollable.

A woman is walking. The
muscles in her legs are
moving in slow gulps.
The gym comes
to my mind and the
smell at the beginning.
          It's
            so
          early.

PART 5

There's a match on
the floor; O bathroom of
stages! The sun burns through
the glass. It fortifies
the density of the leaves
and of your crying
last night.

I saw three girls
passing, going to work,
yet the whole street is
moving away.

The acorns are dry
The acorns are green
on the inside . . . .
            resonant as
                a testicle.

Oh cars, south breeze, two
people standing facing, truck,
baseball bat, swing, lint
flying around,
    go! on on on

Evening,
    I am holding the
ball, evening.

There is a new kite.
It is a bird kite.
It looks like a
bird.

It is made of stretched plastic.
No bird can
fly forever without
moving its wings.
The kite does not move
          its wings.
But there is a noise   coming from it

The electric motor new and
used is not like our brain
here in the darkness,
here in the morning black.
Take-ah, take- ah, tant, tant
          do-ah, do- ah
The bird goes in a tree.
   Bird goes
The bird goes
The pointed wings of
the seagulls
   practice on
pumping the skies.

          Orange soda.
          Distant voices.

   How different each acorn
    is here in his hand
    here in the light, here in the
park   here in the light;
how different each
crumb is here in
          its beak

Washington Square Park, New York City, April 1964

Joseph Ceravolo
1934–1988